BODY SYSTEMS

The Muscular System

by Kay Manolis

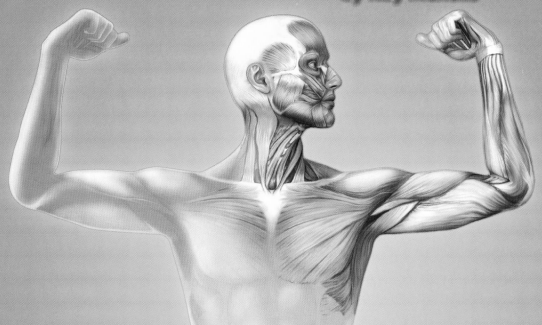

Consultant:
Molly Martin, M.D.
Internal Medicine
MeritCare, Bemidji, MN

BLASTOFF! READERS
4

BELLWETHER MEDIA • MINNEAPOLIS, MN

Note to Librarians, Teachers, and Parents:

Blastoff! Readers are carefully developed by literacy experts and combine standards-based content with developmentally appropriate text.

Level 1 provides the most support through repetition of high-frequency words, light text, predictable sentence patterns, and strong visual support.

Level 2 offers early readers a bit more challenge through varied simple sentences, increased text load, and less repetition of high-frequency words.

Level 3 advances early-fluent readers toward fluency through increased text and concept load, less reliance on visuals, longer sentences, and more literary language.

Level 4 builds reading stamina by providing more text per page, increased use of punctuation, greater variation in sentence patterns, and increasingly challenging vocabulary.

Level 5 encourages children to move from "learning to read" to "reading to learn" by providing even more text, varied writing styles, and less familiar topics.

Whichever book is right for your reader, Blastoff! Readers are the perfect books to build confidence and encourage a love of reading that will last a lifetime!

This edition first published in 2009 by Bellwether Media, Inc.

No part of this publication may be reproduced in whole or in part without written permission of the publisher. For information regarding permission, write to Bellwether Media, Inc., Attention: Permissions Department, Post Office Box 19349, Minneapolis, MN 55419.

Library of Congress Cataloging-in-Publication Data
Manolis, Kay.
  Muscular system / by Kay Manolis.
     p. cm. — (Blastoff! readers: body systems)
  Includes bibliographical references and index.
  Summary: "Introductory text explains the functions and physical concepts of the muscular system with color photography and simple scientific diagrams. Intended for students in grades three through six"–Provided by publisher.
  ISBN-13: 978-1-60014-244-4 (hardcover : alk. paper)
  ISBN-10: 1-60014-244-3 (hardcover : alk. paper)
  1. Muscles–Physiology–Juvenile literature. I. Title.

QP321.M285 2009
612.7'4–dc22   2008032700

Contents

What Is the
Muscular System?

Your body can move in many ways. Some movements are big, like a cartwheel. Some are small, like taking a breath. Either way, your muscular system makes it possible for you to move. Muscles are body parts that can **contract**, or squeeze together, to cause movements.

Kinds of Muscles

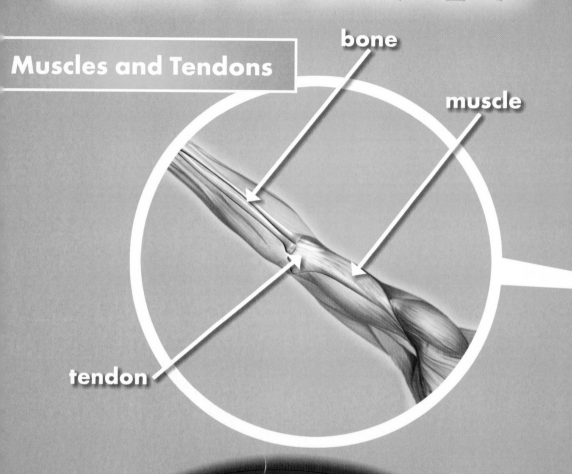

Muscles and Tendons

bone

muscle

tendon

Your body has more than 600 muscles. Most are **skeletal muscles**. They are called skeletal muscles because they work on your skeleton. Strong bands called **tendons** connect skeletal muscles to bones.

6

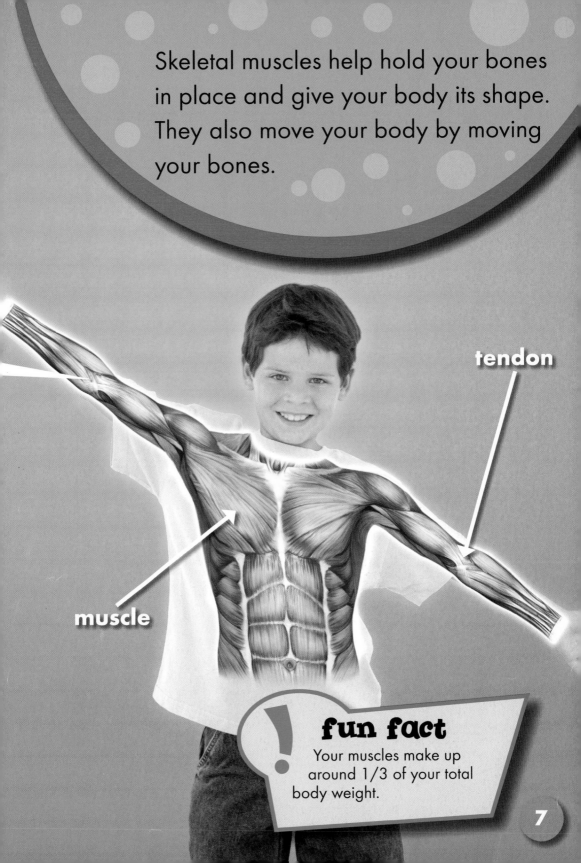

Skeletal muscles help hold your bones in place and give your body its shape. They also move your body by moving your bones.

tendon

muscle

! **fun fact**
Your muscles make up around 1/3 of your total body weight.

Your skeletal muscles, bones, brain, and **nerves** work together to cause most of your body's movements. Nerves are long strings of tissue that carry messages throughout your body. Your brain sends nerve messages to muscles telling them to contract. Muscles pull on bones when they contract. Then bones move.

You decide when you want to move your bones. For this reason, skeletal muscles are also called **voluntary** muscles.

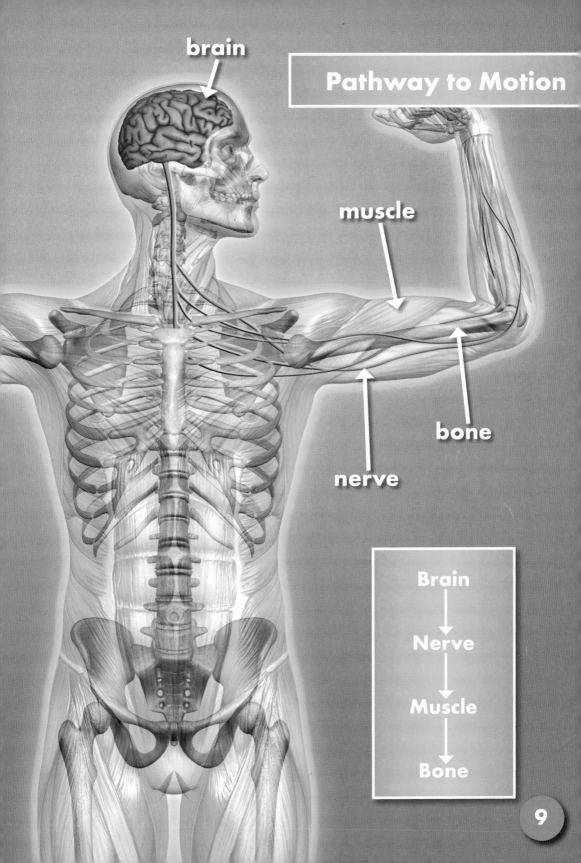

brain

Pathway to Motion

muscle

bone

nerve

Brain
↓
Nerve
↓
Muscle
↓
Bone

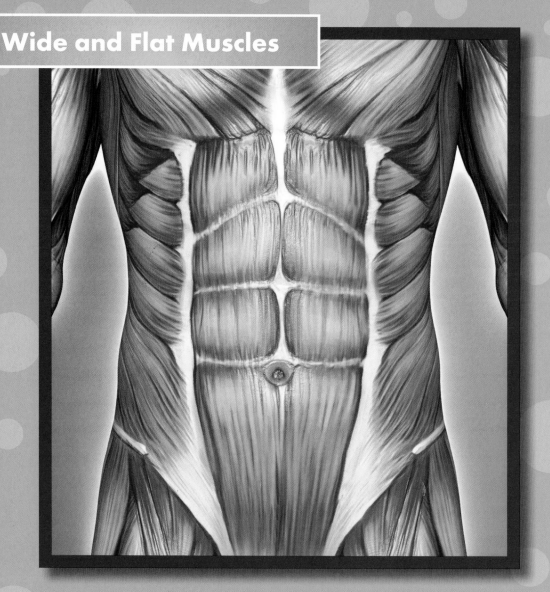

Skeletal muscles come in many shapes and sizes. Some are long bands, like those in your upper arm. Many muscles around the middle of your body are wide and flat. These let you bend and twist. They also help you stand and sit upright.

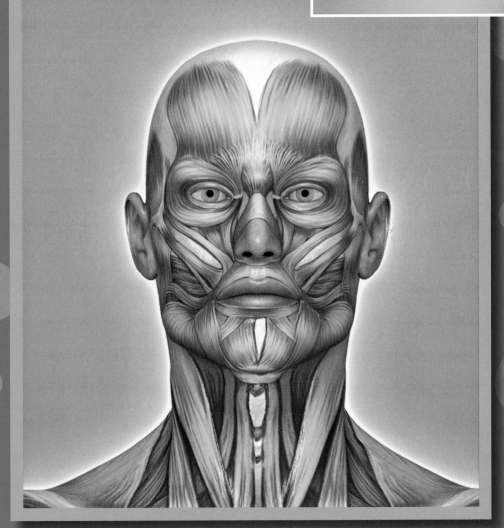

Circular muscles surround your eyes and mouth. They help you close your eyes tightly or squeeze your lips together.

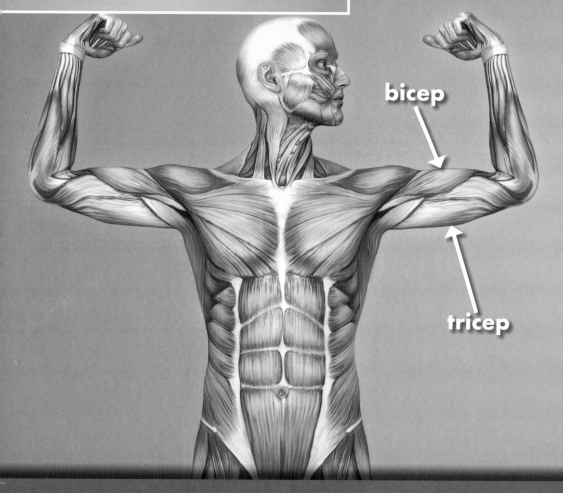

bicep

tricep

Muscles can only pull on your body, they can't push. Most muscles work in pairs. One muscle pulls a bone in one direction. The other pulls in the opposite direction. The muscles in a pair never pull at the same time. When one pulls, the other relaxes.

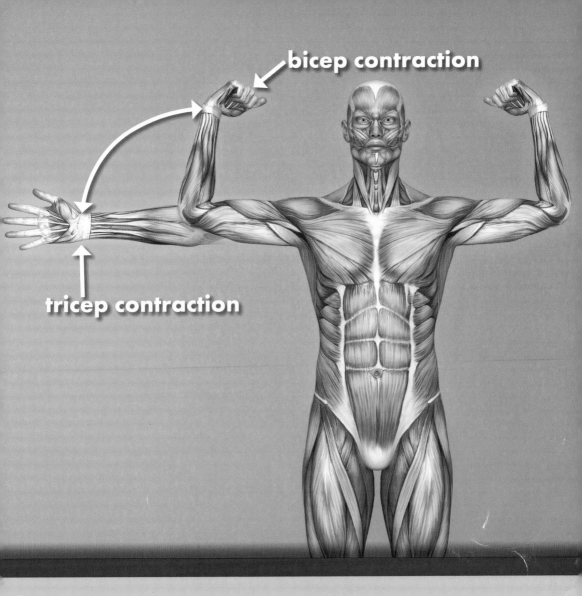

bicep contraction

tricep contraction

The **bicep** and **tricep** are paired muscles in your upper arm. They work together to move your lower arm. The bicep contracts and the tricep relaxes to pull the lower arm toward your body. The tricep contracts and the bicep relaxes to pull the lower arm into a straight position.

13

fun fact

Skeletal muscles get tired after working hard. They must have time to rest.

Most movements require the work of many muscle pairs. For example, you use more than 100 muscles when you walk. Some muscles make your feet push against the ground. Others cause your leg to bend at the knee and then straighten again.

Regular exercise can help muscles gain strength. Strong muscles create a lot of force. Athletes work to build their muscles.

An Example of Smooth Muscle

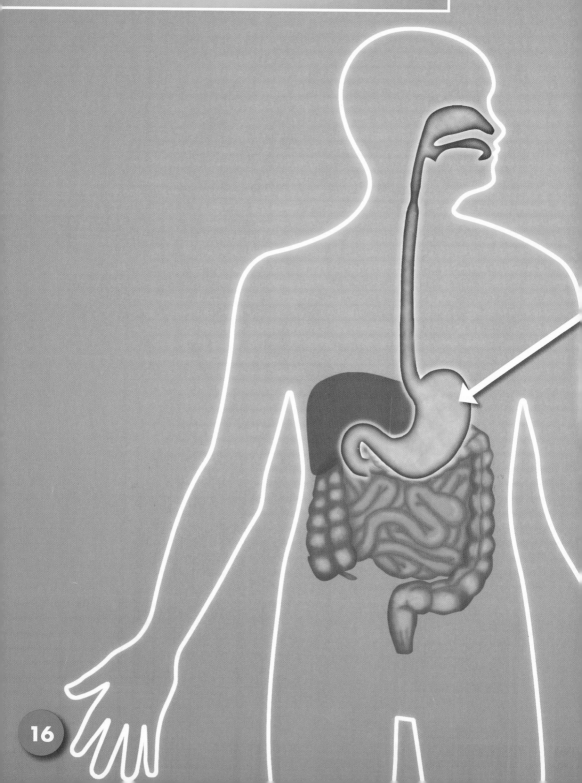

stomach

Your body has different kinds of muscles. Many body **organs** are made of **smooth muscle**. This kind of muscle causes movements inside your body. For example, smooth muscle in the stomach contracts to mix and break down food.

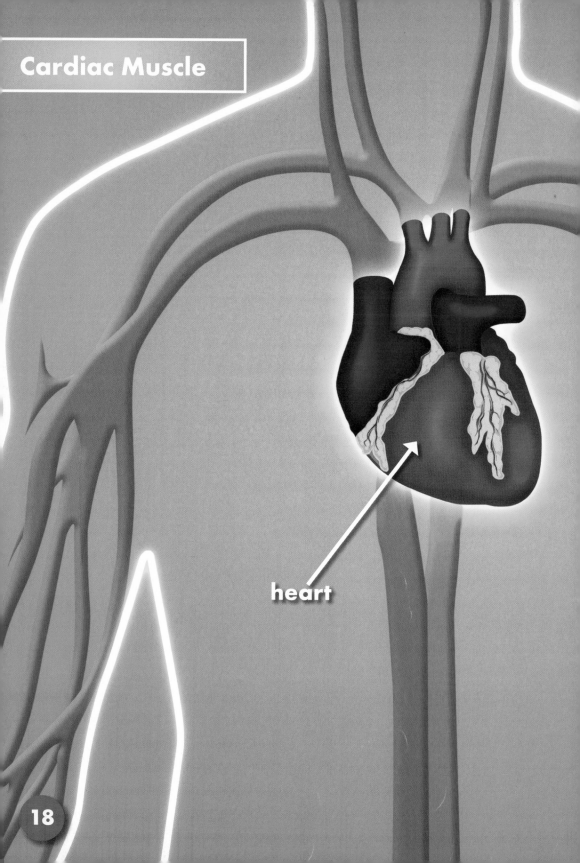

Cardiac Muscle

heart

The heart is made of another kind of muscle called **cardiac muscle**. It pumps blood throughout your body.

Cardiac and smooth muscles are **involuntary** muscles. This means your brain makes them work without you having to think about it. Cardiac and smooth muscles never get tired.

! fun fact

The smallest muscle in the human body is inside the ear. It is smaller than a grain of rice. It helps you to hear by moving a tiny bone in the ear.

Taking Care of Your Muscles

Eating healthy foods is important for your muscles.

Foods with **protein** such as eggs, milk, meat, and nuts help build muscles and keep them healthy. Drinking plenty of water each day also keeps muscles working their best. Take care of your muscular system. You'll be amazed at what it can do!

Glossary

bicep—a muscle in the upper arm; the bicep works with the tricep to move the lower arm.

cardiac muscle—the kind of muscle that makes up the walls of the human heart

contract—to shorten

involuntary—not done by choice

nerves—threads of tissue throughout your body that carry messages between your brain and other parts of your body

organ—a body part that does a certain job to help the body function

protein—a nutrient; proteins are the building blocks of bones, muscles, skin, and blood.

skeletal muscle—the kind of muscle that connects to and moves bones in the body

smooth muscle—the kind of muscle that makes up many of the organs in the body

tendons—bands of tissue that connect muscles to bones

tricep—a muscle in the upper arm; the tricep works with the bicep to move the lower arm.

voluntary—done by choice

To Learn More

AT THE LIBRARY
Ballard, Carol. *How Do We Move?* Austin, Tex.:
Raintree, 1998.

Jakab, Cheryl. *Muscular System.* Mankato, Minn.:
Smart Apple, 2007.

Johnson, Rebecca. *The Muscular System.*
Minneapolis, Minn.: Lerner, 2004.

ON THE WEB
Learning more about the muscular
system is as easy as 1, 2, 3.

1. Go to www.factsurfer.com.

2. Enter "muscular system" into the search box.

3. Click the "Surf" button and you will see a list of
   related Web sites.

With factsurfer.com, finding more information is just a
click away.

Index

The images in this book are reproduced through the courtesy of: Max Delson, front cover, pp. 6, 10, 11, 12, 13; Mandy Godbehear, p. 4; Monkey Business Images / Max Delson, p. 7; Juan Martinez, p. 9; Galyna Andrushko, p. 14; Rich Legg, p. 15; Linda Clavel, pp. 16, 18; Trutta55, p. 20.